God's

Will for
Your Life

DEREK PRINCE

ɯ
WHITAKER
HOUSE

GOD'S WILL FOR YOUR LIFE

Derek Prince
Derek Prince Ministries International
P. O. Box 19501
Charlotte, NC 28219

ISBN: 0-88368-408-X
Printed in the United States of America
© 1986 by Derek Prince Ministries International

Whitaker House
30 Hunt Valley Circle
New Kensington, PA 15068

Library of Congress Cataloging-in-Publication Data

Prince, Derek.
  God's will for your life / by Derek Prince.
     p. cm.
  ISBN 0-88368-408-X (pbk. : alk. paper)
  1. God—Will. 2. Christian life. I. Title.
  BV4501.3 .P748 2002
  248.4—dc21

                              2002002052

1 2 3 4 5 6 7 8 9 10 11 12 / 09 08 07 06 05 04 03 02

Contents

─♦─

1. Jesus, Our Pattern 7

2. The Outworking of God's Will 17

3. Further Outworking of God's Will 25

4. The Culmination: The Cross 35

5. Following the Example of Jesus 47

About the Author 59

1

Jesus, Our Pattern

1

Jesus, Our Pattern

❦

The subject of this book is related in a very personal and practical way to the life of each one of us—*God's Will for Your Life.*

Let us begin by asking a personal question: Do you have a known, clear objective for your life? Or are you drifting through life, being carried here and there by the winds of habit and fashion, tossed by waves of circumstances over which you have no control?

There is nothing more tragic in a human life than aimlessness. If you aim at nothing, you may be sure you will hit it. You may have talent, intelligence, and special abilities, but without an objective your life will end in frustration, because you will have accomplished very little of permanent value.

Herein lies one of the greatest benefits and blessings of the Christian life. As God planned it, the Christian life gives each one of us an objective for living. This objective for living is provided for us by our faith in Christ.

The first picture of the Christian life and its objective that we will look at is found in Hebrews:

> *Therefore, since we are surrounded by such a great cloud of witnesses, let us throw off everything that hinders and the sin that so easily entangles, and let us run with perseverance the race marked out for us. Let us fix our eyes on Jesus, the author and perfecter of our faith, who for the joy set before him endured the cross, scorning its shame, and sat down at the right hand of the throne of God.*
> (Hebrews 12:1–2)

There are three important truths mentioned here. First, the Christian life is a race marked out for us in advance. We do not need to mark the course out; that has been done for us. We need only to run the race. However, this race is not a dash or a sprint, but it is much more like a long-distance marathon.

To be able to run this long race, we must throw off everything that hinders us or gets in our way. These things may not always be sinful; nevertheless, they keep us from running the race. For that reason we must eliminate them from our lives.

In this race, there is a particular quality that is emphasized: *perseverance* or *endurance*. For us to finish the race, it will require our perseverance or endurance.

Second, we are to fix our eyes on Jesus. Jesus is our pattern and our inspiration. If we take our eyes off Jesus for any length of time, we will lose our ability to run the race successfully.

Third, Jesus is *"the author and perfecter of our faith."* He is the one who set it all in motion. We may recognize that He is the author of our faith, but we often lose sight of the fact that He is also the perfecter. Jesus not only started it, He is going to complete it.

Both in Scripture and in God's dealings in my life, I have seen that He never starts anything He is not capable of finishing. We need to take heart and be encouraged by this fact. Jesus started us on this race, and He is going to enable us to finish it. He is the author and the perfecter.

Keep these three important things in mind. First, the Christian life is a race in which the course is marked out ahead of us, and it is going to take endurance to complete the race. Second, to be successful we must fix our eyes on Jesus. He is both our pattern and our inspiration. Third, He is both the author and perfecter of our faith. As long as we keep our eyes on Jesus, He will not merely set us going, but He will enable us to keep going and bring us successfully and triumphantly to the finish of the race.

In looking to Jesus as both our pattern and our inspiration in this Christian race, we see that the key to His success was His motivation. Unless we really understand His motivation and enter into it with Him, we will find this race too much for us.

In Hebrews 10:5–10, the writer quotes from Psalm 40 and then applies it to Jesus Christ.

Therefore, when Christ came into the world, he said: "Sacrifice and offering you did not desire, but a body you prepared for me; with burnt offerings and sin offerings you were not pleased. Then I said, 'Here I am—it is written about me in the scroll—I have come to do your will, O God.'" First he said, "Sacrifices and offerings, burnt offerings and sin offerings you did not desire, nor were you pleased with them" (although the law required them to be made). Then he said, "Here I am, I have come to do your will." He sets aside the first to establish the second. And by that will, we have been made holy through the sacrifice of the body of Jesus Christ once for all.

(Hebrews 10:5–10)

Notice the word *"body"* at the beginning. The Lord says, *"Sacrifice and offering you did not desire, but a body you prepared for me."* At the end the comment is: *"By that will* [the will of God done by Jesus Christ], *we have been made holy through the sacrifice of the body of Jesus Christ once for all."* God provided Jesus with a body to sacrifice on our behalf. This theme is going to follow all through this study.

From this passage we see, first, what Jesus' supreme motivation was: *"I have come to do your will."* That statement was quoted twice for emphasis so it would not be missed. The paramount purpose and single objective of Jesus throughout His earthly life was to do the will of God. He was absolutely clear about it, and He never swerved from it.

Second, in connection with the first, there was a part written for Jesus to play: *"Here I am—it is written about me in the scroll—I have come to do your will, O God."* It was written in the scroll of God's Word before He came. Jesus did not write His own part or improvise on the script He was given. He discovered it through studying the Scriptures.

Third, God's will for Jesus culminated in the sacrifice of Jesus' own body. God's purpose and plan in giving Him a body was that Jesus would offer His body as the perfect sacrifice on behalf of mankind.

Note the following three points:

1. Jesus' supreme motivation was to do God's will.

2. There was a part for Him already written in the scroll of Scripture.

3. God's will for Jesus culminated in the sacrifice of His own body.

Jesus, Our Pattern

Each of these three points must have its counterpart in our lives. Every one of those statements that was true about Jesus should be true about us. Each one of us needs the same motivation Jesus had to do God's will and to discover what is written for us in the scroll of Scripture. Finally, the doing of God's will in our lives will culminate in the sacrifice of our own bodies.

2

The
Outworking
of God's Will

2

The Outworking
of God's Will

O ne essential condition for a successful life is to have a clearly defined and steadily pursued objective. Without such an objective a person is like a boat drifting on the open sea, carried here and there by the winds of habit and the waves of circumstance, without any control over his or her own destiny.

As I stated earlier, one of the greatest benefits and blessings of the Christian life is that it provides each one of us with an objective for living. In this respect, Jesus is both our pattern and our inspiration.

Let us look at how the commitment to do God's will was practically worked out in the earthly life and ministry of Jesus. We will begin with the well-known incident where Jesus met the woman of Samaria at Jacob's Well.

Jesus and His disciples were journeying by foot, back from Judea to Galilee. They passed through Samaria and came to the place that is still known today as Jacob's Well. Jesus was tired and sat down by the well to rest. Apparently they had run out of food and were hungry, because the disciples had gone into the local town to buy food. Then the woman from Samaria came out to the well, and Jesus had that wonderful conversation with her in which He gave her that beautiful promise about the living water for everyone who was thirsty. The woman became so excited that she left her water pot without collecting water and went back into the town to tell the men about this wonderful person she had met at the well.

The Outworking of God's Will

As Jesus remained at the well, His disciples came back and found Him sitting there. This is what follows in the account in John's gospel:

> *Meanwhile his disciples urged him, "Rabbi, eat something." But he said to them, "I have food to eat that you know nothing about." Then his disciples said to each other, "Could someone have brought him food?" "My food," said Jesus, "is to do the will of him who sent me and to finish his work. Do you not say, 'Four months more and then the harvest'? I tell you, open your eyes and look at the fields! They are ripe for harvest. Even now the reaper draws his wages, even now he harvests the crop for eternal life, so that the sower and the reaper may be glad together."* (John 4:31–36)

Here is the clear statement of Jesus: *"My food...is to do the will of him who sent me."* The central motivation of His entire earthly life was always to do the will of the One who sent Him. There are two results of this motivation in the life of Jesus that should have their counterpart in our lives.

First, Jesus' commitment to do the will of God actually worked supernatural, physical restoration in Him. When He came to the well, He was tired and hungry. Jesus sat down, but instead of eating, He flowed in the will of God in His conversation with this needy woman. In putting God's will above His own physical needs, He received supernatural restoration. When the disciples came with food, Jesus was not particularly interested. He said, "I have already eaten." His disciples could not understand what kind of food He could have had.

Jesus explained, *"My food...is to do the will of him who sent me and to finish his work."* Food is the thing that gives us physical strength and sustains us. Jesus said, "That is what sustains Me and keeps Me going—My commitment to do the will of the One who sent Me."

Second, Jesus had a different viewpoint. He began to speak about how to look at the world. He said, "You look at the world one way; I look at the world another. You say there are four more months to harvest, but for Me the harvest field is already ripe. I am already reaping." Jesus was referring to His encounter with the Samaritan woman. He was reaping the harvest in that village at that very moment. A few minutes later, the woman came back with all the men in the village, and Jesus shared with them.

The disciples looked at things from a purely natural point of view. They said, "It is not yet time for harvest." In contrast, Jesus had a spiritual viewpoint. He saw things from another perspective. Jesus' commitment to do the will of God was what gave Him this spiritual insight.

Approximately two-thirds of the way through the next chapter of John's gospel, we find another statement Jesus made that has much to teach us about the result of being committed to doing God's will. Jesus is discussing the healing of a man who had been paralyzed for many years. In the middle of this discussion, Jesus makes this statement:

> *I can do nothing on My own initiative. As I hear, I judge; and My judgment is just, because I do not seek My own will, but the will of Him who sent Me.*
>
> (John 5:30 NAS)

Notice Jesus' words, *"My judgment is just."* In other words, Jesus was saying, "My judgment is right." Why? *"Because I do not seek My own will, but the will of Him who sent Me."*

Here we find a third result of that commitment to do the will of God. I would call it "just judgment" or "impartial discernment."

Jesus was never fooled. Nobody ever deceived Him. Jesus discerned the truth in everyone who came to Him. He saw into their inner motives and knew what they were really after. Jesus knew how to reach and touch them where they needed to be touched, whether it was spiritually or physically, because of His commitment to doing God's will.

How can we avoid foolish judgment and wrong appraisals of people and situations? We find the key in John 5:30, where Jesus said, "My judgment is just; My discernment is accurate. I see things the way they really are." Why? *"Because I do not seek My own will, but the will of Him who sent Me."*

Jesus' judgment was not clouded by His desire to get His own way. He was in neutral, so to speak, until the Father moved Him. Jesus waited for the Father's revelation of His will, and then Jesus made a just and accurate judgment.

3

Further Outworking of God's Will

3

Further Outworking of God's Will

So far, we have looked at the way in which Jesus' commitment to do God's will was practically worked out in His earthly life and ministry. I pointed out three specific results in His life. First, there was physical restoration. At Jacob's Well He was tired and hungry, yet in doing the will of God by sharing the truth with that Samaritan woman, received physical restoration. He was no longer hungry when His disciples returned with food.

, there was a proper view of the situation. Jesus saw the harvest field with the eyes of God, while His disciples still looked with natural eyes. Jesus' commitment to do the will of God gave Him a view that differed from the perspectives of those around Him.

, there was just judgment or impartial discernment. Jesus said, *"My judgment is just, because I do not seek My own will, but the will of Him who sent Me"* (John 5:30 NAS). He was never fooled or carried away by His own wishful thinking, emotions, or reactions. Jesus always waited for the Father's revelation concerning every situation.

us continue by looking at two further results of Jesus' commitment to do the will of God. We are going to look at the discourse of Jesus after He fed the five thousand with five loaves and two fishes, and specifically at the spiritual application to Himself.

Then Jesus declared, "I am the bread of life. He who comes to me will never go hungry, and he who believes in me will never be thirsty. But as I told you, you have seen me and still you do not believe. All that the Father gives me will come to me, and whoever comes to me I will never drive away. For I have come down from heaven not to do my will but to do the will of him who sent me. [It is significant that there must be a setting aside of our own will before we can do the will of God.] *And this is the will of him who sent me, that I shall lose none of all that he has given me, but raise them up at the last day. For my Father's will is that everyone who looks to the Son and believes in him shall have eternal life, and I will raise him up at the last day."* (John 6:35–40)

Jesus had set aside His own will and, at the end of His discourse, He referred to *"my Father's will."* I never read that statement, *"I am the bread of life,"* without being moved. *"Everyone who looks to* [Me] *and believes in* [Me] *shall have eternal life, and I will raise him up at the last day."* What a beautiful offer from the One who can feed and give life to a hungry, dying world!

But what was the price Jesus had to pay? It was, "Not doing My will, but the will of Him who sent Me." As long as we are busy with our own plans, purposes, and objectives, we cannot be channels of divine life. Since this was true even of Jesus, how much more so is it for you and me? If we want the privilege of being God's bread, broken to feed a hungry world, then we must make a renunciation: *"Not...my will but... the will of him who sent me."*

This was Paul's personal testimony in his second letter to the Corinthians:

> *We always carry around in our body the death of Jesus, so that the life of Jesus may also be revealed in our body. For we who are alive are always being given over to death for Jesus' sake, so that his life may be revealed in our mortal body. So then, death is at work in us, but life is at work in you.* (2 Corinthians 4:10–12)

Paul explained, *"So then, death is at work in us, but life is at work in you."* The world needs channels of life, but there is a price to pay. If you want to be a channel of life to others, death has first to work in you. We cannot have it any other way or change the order.

The pattern is clear: when death is at work in you, then life is at work in others. You are here not to do your own will, but to do the will of Him who sent you. The will of Him who sent you is to feed and give life to a hungry and dying world. If you will renounce your own will and pursue with single-hearted devotion the will of God as revealed for your life, then you, too, in your own measure, can be food for a hungry world and life to a dying world. However, this is not possible while you are concerned with doing your own will.

There was one more result produced in the life of Jesus by His commitment to do the will of the Father. We can discover it in Jesus' great high-priestly prayer to the Father on behalf of His disciples before He was separated from them. This beautiful expression of Christ is found in the latter part of the gospel of John:

> *I glorified Thee on the earth, having accomplished the work which Thou hast given Me to do.* (John 17:4 NAS)

Where this version says, *"accomplished,"* it is a translation of a form of the Greek word, *teleios,* which also means "to finish" or "to complete." *"I glorified Thee on the earth, having* [finished] *the work which Thou hast given Me to do."* Throughout the Gospels, the emphasis of Jesus was not merely on doing the will of God, but on finishing the work. In connection with the incident of the Samaritan woman at Jacob's Well, He had said, *"My food is to do the will of Him who sent Me, and to finish His work"* (John 4:34 NKJV).

Jesus was always looking ahead to the triumphant conclusion of His task. Here He says, "Now I have brought glory to You, O Father, on the earth, because I have come to the end of the work. I have finished it." Returning to the picture of a race we considered previously, we could say that Jesus is finishing the race. He is just about to breast the tape, and, in doing that, He says, "I have brought glory to God."

Doing the will of God will always bring glory to Him. Whatever task God calls you to do, if you do it thoroughly and finish it, you can bring glory to Him. The task God assigns to you may be simple, humble, or ordinary. It may entail being the best wife and mother, a godly husband and father, an efficient secretary, or a good businessman. Whatever the task, if you finish it and do a thorough job, you will bring glory to God.

Self-seeking, halfhearted service never glorifies God. One of the reasons it does not is that such a person's motive for serving is always wrapped up in himself or herself. There are Christians, even ministers, who are concerned for their own glory rather than God's glory. They may attract large followings and get people interested in their gifts and ministries, but the ultimate end will not be the glory of God.

In order to glorify God, we must have a single vision for the task God has assigned us. In addition, we need to have a fixed determination that we will finish the task no matter what it costs. There is nothing I desire more than to come to the end of my ministry and life here on Earth and be able to say in my own limited measure, *"I glorified Thee on the earth, having accomplished the work which Thou hast given Me to do."*

4

The Culmination: The Cross

4

The Culmination: The Cross

-~3+3~-

We have been taking Jesus as both the pattern and the inspiration for living. We have seen that the supreme motivation of His life was to do God's will as revealed in the scroll of Scripture. Our key verse is this:

> Then [Jesus] *said, "Here I am—it is writ-*
> *ten about me in the scroll—I have come*
> *to do your will, O God."* (Hebrews 10:7)

God's Will for Your Life

Two vital points are evident: first, the motive for which Jesus came was to do God's will; second, the part He had to play was already written in the scroll. That should also be true of you and me.

We have also looked at five specific results in the earthly life of Jesus that came about through His commitment to do the will of God:

1. He received physical restoration in a supernatural way.

2. He had a proper view of the situation He was in, different from that of the people around Him.

3. He rendered just judgment or impartial discernment. (Jesus was never gullible or deceived. He always saw exactly how a thing really was.)

4. He was a channel of life to a dying world.

5. He glorified God on the earth.

As He attained all these results, Jesus set the pattern for us to follow.

Let us continue by looking at the culmination of God's will in the life of Jesus. In

the tenth chapter of Hebrews, we discover that
God's supreme will for Jesus was the sacrifice
of His body:

> *Therefore, when Christ came into the*
> *world, he said: "Sacrifice and offering*
> *you did not desire, but a body you pre-*
> *pared for me; with burnt offerings and*
> *sin offerings you were not pleased. Then*
> *I said, 'Here I am—it is written about*
> *me in the scroll—I have come to do your*
> *will, O God.'" First he said, "Sacrifices*
> *and offerings, burnt offerings and sin*
> *offerings you did not desire, nor were you*
> *pleased with them" (although the law*
> *required them to be made). Then he said,*
> *"Here I am, I have come to do your will."*
> *He sets aside the first to establish the*
> *second. And by that will, we have been*
> *made holy through the sacrifice of the*
> *body of Jesus Christ once for all.*
>
> (Hebrews 10:5–10)

Jesus came to this world to do the will of
His Father. In order to do God's will, God prepared a body for Him. The outworking of that
will demanded that Jesus sacrifice His own
body. The culmination or ultimate goal of the
life of Jesus was to sacrifice His body on behalf
of the world.

As we have seen, there was a continual emphasis in the mind of Jesus, not merely to do God's work, but to finish it and complete God's will. The nearer Jesus came to the end of His earthly ministry, the stronger this emphasis became in His life.

Let us look at a statement in the gospel of Luke:

And it came about, when the days were approaching for His ascension [literally, "His 'taking up,'" which refers to Jesus being taken up through His death on the cross], *that He resolutely set His face to go to Jerusalem.* (Luke 9:51 NAS)

Notice that key phrase, *"He resolutely set His face."* Jesus knew what lay ahead of Him. He had already told His disciples, although they refused to believe Him. As the time of completion approached, *"He resolutely set His face."* He was determined to finish His work.

The prophet Isaiah, by the Spirit of Christ, prophetically foretold the culmination of the life of Jesus on the earth as follows:

The Sovereign LORD has given me an instructed tongue [a disciple's tongue—Jesus was the disciple of the Father], *to*

*know the word that sustains the weary.
He wakens me morning by morning,
wakens my ear to listen like one being
taught.* (Isaiah 50:4)

Jesus was always in the school of discipleship with the Father. At the beginning of each day, as Jesus spent time in prayer, He received His directions for that day when He heard the Father's voice speak to Him.

Continuing in Isaiah, we read:

*The Sovereign LORD has opened my ears,
and I have not been rebellious; I have not
drawn back. I offered my back to those
who beat me, my cheeks to those who
pulled out my beard; I did not hide my
face from mocking and spitting.*
(Isaiah 50:5–6)

It is very important to see that Jesus gave His back to those who beat Him. He freely gave it because it was the Father's will and direction. He heard the Father tell Him, "That's what I sent You to do, My Son," and so He did not withhold Himself. He gave Himself over to His torturers.

Finishing the passage in Isaiah, we find:

Because the Sovereign LORD helps me, I will not be disgraced. Therefore have I set my face like flint, and I know I will not be put to shame. (Isaiah 50:7)

Luke said, *"He resolutely set His face."* Prophetically writing seven hundred years earlier, Isaiah said, *"Therefore have I set my face like flint."* Jesus knew what He was going to endure. In fact, it is written in the previous verses of Isaiah, *"I offered my back to those who beat me, my cheeks to those who pulled out my beard; I did not hide my face from mocking and spitting."*

In effect Jesus said in His heart, "I have set My face like a flint. No matter what lies ahead, I'm going to go through with it because My purpose is to do the work that God has assigned to Me and to finish it."

Now we come to the actual culmination of the earthly life of Jesus. Jesus had been on the cross for three hours or more, and He was nearing His end. We read in the gospel of John:

Later, knowing that all was now completed, and so that the Scripture would be fulfilled, Jesus said, "I am thirsty." A jar of wine vinegar was there, so they soaked a sponge in it, put the sponge on a stalk of the hyssop plant, and lifted it to Jesus' lips. When he had received the drink, Jesus said, "It is finished." With that, he bowed his head and gave up his spirit. (John 19:28–30)

Jesus released His own spirit to the Father (Luke 23:46). He had told His disciples earlier,

Therefore My Father loves Me, because I lay down My life that I may take it again. No one takes it from Me, but I lay it down of Myself. I have power to lay it down, and I have power to take it again. This command I have received from My Father. (John 10:17–18 NKJV)

Before Jesus dismissed His spirit, one of His last great utterances was: *"It is finished"* (John 19:30). *What* was finished? He had finished the task of His earthly assignment. Throughout His life He had been saying, *"My food...is to do the will of him who sent me and to finish his work"* (John 4:34). Then, in anticipation of this moment, in His prayer, which is found in the seventeenth chapter of John, He expressed, "I have glorified You on Earth. I have finished the work You gave Me to do." On the cross it was actually fulfilled as He cried out, *"It is finished."*

That was not a cry of defeat. That was a cry of triumph! "*'It is finished!'* Everything that was assigned to Me I have done. I have done it completely. I have left nothing out. Now redemption is available through My sacrifice there on the cross!"

In Greek, *"It is finished!"* is just one word, *tetelestai.* It is the perfect tense of a verb that means "to complete something," "to finish something," "to do something perfectly." In searching for a way to communicate it in English, I thought of such phrases as these: "It is completely complete," "It is perfectly perfect," and "Everything that had to be done (for man's redemption through the sacrifice of My body) has been done."

Jesus would not release His spirit until He could say, *"It is finished,"* and until He knew that He had done everything required of Him by the Father. That was the goal toward which His life was directed. That was the supreme motivation that had caused Him to set His face like a flint and had enabled Him to go through the shame, pain, rejection, and disgrace.

The Culmination: The Cross

I have often heard it said that it was not the nails that held Jesus to the cross, but rather it was His commitment to the Father's will. That commitment was something from which He would not swerve or turn to the right or to the left. To do His Father's will no matter what was Jesus' motivation. That was His purpose in living here on Earth.

God had given Jesus a body. He knew from the Scriptures that God's purpose for His body was that He should sacrifice it on the cross on behalf of mankind. Everything Jesus did was directed to the fulfillment of the will of God and the completion of His assignment.

5

Following
the Example
of Jesus

5

Following the Example of Jesus

※

We have been consistently looking to Jesus as both our pattern and our inspiration. We have seen that the commitment to do God's will was the motivation that brought Jesus down from heaven to Earth. This commitment shaped and directed the entire course of His earthly life and ministry and culminated in the sacrifice of His own body on the cross.

God's Will for Your Life

Let us consider how we can apply this example of Jesus to our own lives. Three main steps are necessary in applying the pattern Jesus gave us. The first step is to will to do God's will. The apostle John recorded that Jesus said:

> *If anyone chooses to do God's will, he will find out whether my teaching comes from God or whether I speak on my own.*
> (John 7:17)

The Greek word that is translated here as *"chooses"* is actually a form of the verb, *thelo,* which means "to will" or "to determine." If anyone chooses to do God's will or if anybody wills to do God's will, he or she will find out whether Jesus speaks on His own.

Many religious people underestimate the function of the will in their spiritual lives. Many people's lives are directed by impressions, feelings, and promptings. However, the thing that ultimately determines the direction of our lives is the exercise of our wills. That is the decisive factor. We cannot lead a right life if we do not will to lead a right life.

Jesus sets before us this challenge, which is also an invitation: will you set your will to do God's will? Without meeting that challenge, leading a right life will never happen. It does not come about by inspiration, wonderful preaching, or somebody praying for us.

There must come a point in our lives where we make a personal decision. *Decision* is a key word. We have to decide: "I am going to do God's will." Jesus told us, *"If anyone chooses to do God's will,* [then] *he will find out whether my teaching comes from God."*

It is important to understand that we do not find out first and then will to do God's will; we first choose to do, and then we find out. Many people have the order wrong. They pray, "God, show me the whole thing. I want to understand it all first, and then I will decide to do what You tell me." However, that is not how it works. God does not scratch an itching intellect. If you just want to know out of your intellectual curiosity without the willingness to make a commitment, God will not reveal His will to you. But if you will to do God's will, then understanding, insight, and revelation will follow.

Let me put it another way: commitment leads to understanding, not understanding to commitment. You do not first understand God's will and then commit yourself to do it. You commit yourself to do God's will; then, to your committed mind, God begins to unfold His will. All of us come to a point in our lives where we must make a vital decision for ourselves: "My decision is to do God's will." We cannot say "if" or "perhaps." That is not a commitment.

The second step is the sacrifice of our bodies. The doing of God's will culminated for Jesus in the sacrifice of His body. He knew that when He set out to do God's will. It may surprise you to know—but it is very clearly stated in Scripture—that for you and me to do God's will requires, likewise, the sacrifice of our bodies. However, there is a difference. The sacrifice of the body of Jesus meant its death. We are told by Paul to sacrifice our living bodies:

> Therefore, I urge you, brothers, in view of God's mercy, to offer your bodies as living sacrifices, holy and pleasing to God—this is your spiritual act of worship.　　　　　(Romans 12:1)

In essence, God says to each of us, "In the light of all that I have done for you, the response I require is for you to offer your body to Me as a living sacrifice. Place your body on

My altar. Make your body available to Me without reservation."

If you offer your body as a living sacrifice
to God, you no longer claim ownership of your
body. You no longer decide where your body
will go or what your body will do, eat, or wear.
You have given up the right to make those deci-
sions. From now on, your body belongs to God.
You have sacrificed it to Him, a living body, on
His altar.

Whatever is placed on the altar of God
belongs thereafter to God. It no longer belongs
to the person who gave it. God requires that
we, just like Jesus, sacrifice our bodies. The
difference is that Jesus sacrificed His body
through death, but we are asked to sacrifice
our bodies while they are still alive. We are to
hand our bodies over to God and give up our
rights and our claims to them.

That may sound very frightening, but I want
to tell you that it is very exciting. Somehow, we
picture that what this means is that we will end
up in some lonely wasteland, wearing rags and
living on bread and water, but that is not what
God has in mind.

"For I know the plans that I have for you,"
declares the LORD, "plans for welfare and

> *not for calamity to give you a future and a*
> *hope."*   (Jeremiah 29:11 NAS)

God has all sorts of ideas about what He might do with you and your body, but He is not going to tell you until your body belongs to Him. You must commit it to Him first; then you will be given understanding.

After offering our bodies as living sacrifices, we come to the next step, which is renewing the mind. Paul described this very clearly in Romans:

> *Do not conform any longer to the pattern*
> *of this world, but be transformed by the*
> *renewing of your mind. Then you will be*
> *able to test and approve what God's will*
> *is—his good, pleasing and perfect will.*
>   (Romans 12:2)

Once you have taken the decisive step of handing your body over to God as a living sacrifice, something happens in your mind. That decision releases something in your mind, and it becomes renewed. You no longer think the way the world thinks. Worldly people are self-centered in their thinking. "If I do this, how will it affect me? If I say this, will I get a raise? Will I be promoted? Will people like me?" It all centers around "me." But the renewed mind centers around God. "Will this glorify God? Is this God's purpose in my life?"

"With the mind thus renewed," Paul explained to us, "then you can find out the will of God." God will not give that revelation until you have made the commitment. The commitment leads to the renewing of your mind. With your mind renewed, you can discern the will of God and find the path God has for you in life.

In most cases God's path for you will be very different from what you think it might be. The Devil will be right there on your shoulder, whispering in your ear that God's way is going to be miserable and hard. Satan will tell you that you are going to spend the rest of your life washing dishes or living somewhere in a desert. That could be true but, most probably, it will not be that way. However, you will never know until you make the commitment.

The outworking of this surrender of your body to God will be the same as it was in the life of Jesus. There were five results of this determination in the life of Jesus, and you can anticipate the same results in your life when you surrender your body and your will to God.

1. There was supernatural, physical restoration. Jesus was not limited to His own physical strength, nor will you be if you are committed to the will of God.

2. There was proper vision. Jesus saw things the way God sees things, and so will you when you are committed to the will of God.

3. There was just judgment or clear discernment. Jesus was not fooled, and He was not deceived. He saw things in people the way they really were.

4. Jesus became a channel of life to a dying world. Likewise, you and I can be channels of life when we are committed to doing God's will.

5. Jesus said, *"I have glorified You on the earth. I have finished the work which You have given Me to do"* (John 17:4 NKJV). If we will commit ourselves to God and His will and to finishing it with all our hearts, we, too, will be able to glorify God on the earth.

When you totally surrender your body and your will to God, yielding any further claim of self-control to Him, you will glorify the Lord and find deep peace and personal

Following the Example of Jesus

satisfaction in your soul. You will discover a new sense of purpose as God reveals His will for your life.

About the
Author

About the Author

---⚜---

Derek Prince was born in India of British parents. He was educated as a scholar of Greek and Latin at two of Britain's most famous educational institutions—Eton College and Cambridge University. From 1940 to 1949, he held a Fellowship (equivalent to a resident professorship) in ancient and modern philosophy at King's College, Cambridge. He also studied Hebrew and Aramaic, both at Cambridge University and at the Hebrew University in Jerusalem. In addition, he speaks a number of modern languages.

In the early years of World War II, while serving as a hospital attendant with the British Army, Derek experienced a life-changing encounter with Jesus Christ, concerning which he writes:

> Out of this encounter, I formed two conclusions which I have never since had reason to change: first, that Jesus Christ is alive; second, that the Bible is a true, relevant, up-to-date book. These two conclusions radically and permanently altered the whole course of my life.

Since then, Derek has devoted his life to studying and teaching God's Word. His primary gift is explaining the Bible and its teachings in a clear and simple way, so that people everywhere can find relevance for their lives.

Derek Prince's nondenominational, nonsectarian approach has opened doors for his teaching to people from many different racial and religious backgrounds, and he is internationally recognized as one of the leading Bible expositors of our time. His daily radio broadcast, *Today with Derek Prince*, reaches more than half the globe, as it is translated into Arabic, five Chinese languages (Mandarin, Amoy, Cantonese, Shanghaiese, Swatow), Malagasy, Mongolian, Spanish, Russian, and

About the Author

Tongan. He has published more than forty books, which have been translated into more than sixty foreign languages.

Through the Global Outreach Leaders Program of Derek Prince Ministries, his books and audio cassettes are sent free of charge to hundreds of national Christian leaders in the Third World, Eastern Europe, and Russia.

Now past the age of seventy-five, Derek Prince still travels the world—imparting God's revealed truth, praying for the sick and afflicted, and sharing his prophetic insight into world events in the light of Scripture.

The international base of Derek Prince Ministries is located in Charlotte, North Carolina, with branch offices in Australia, Canada, Germany, Holland, New Zealand, South Africa, and the United Kingdom.

OTHER POWERFUL Books

from Whitaker House

Spiritual Warfare
Derek Prince

Derek Prince explains the battle that's happening now between the forces of God and the forces of evil. Choose to be prepared by learning the enemy's strategies so you can effectively block his attack. With God on our side, nothing will keep us from victory.

ISBN: 0-88368-670-8 • Trade • 144 pages

The Grace of Yielding
Derek Prince

If God asked you, as He did with Abraham, to sacrifice your "pride and joy," your "Isaac," could you? From the Scriptures, Derek Prince shows that God will give back to you abundantly when you are willing to yield to Him.

ISBN: 0-88368-693-7 • Trade • 96 pages

God's Plan for Your Money
Derek Prince

God has a plan for all aspects of your life, including your finances. In this book, Derek Prince reveals how to handle your money according to biblical principles so that you may live in God's blessing and abundance.

ISBN: 0-88368-707-0 • Trade • 96 pages